Ronald Reagan's
WISDOM
for the Twenty-First Century

Ronald Reagan's
WISDOM
for the Twenty-First Century

Commentary by John E. Wade II & Daniel P. Agatino
Edited by Charlotte Livingston

PELICAN PUBLISHING COMPANY
Gretna 2012

The word "Pelican" and the depiction of a pelican are
trademarks of Pelican Publishing Company, Inc., and are
registered in the U.S. Patent and Trademark Office.

Library of Congress Cataloging-in-Publication Data

Reagan, Ronald.
Ronald Reagan's wisdom for the twenty-first century / commentary
by John E. Wade II and Daniel P. Agatino ; edited by Charlotte
Livingston.
  p. cm.
  ISBN 978-1-4556-1706-7 (pbk. : alk. paper) — ISBN 978-1-4556-
1707-4 (e-book) 1. Reagan, Ronald—Quotations. 2. United States—
Politics and government—1981-1989—Anecdotes. 3. Quotations,
American. I. Wade, John E., II. II. Agatino, Daniel Philip Alexander.
III. Livingston, Charlotte. IV. Title.
  E838.5.R432 2012a
  973.927092—dc23
                                            2012006787

Printed in the United States of America
Published by Pelican Publishing Company, Inc.
1000 Burmaster Street, Gretna, Louisiana 70053

TABLE OF CONTENTS

INTRODUCTION

Pres. Ronald Reagan is remembered as the "Great Communicator." This book presents typical examples of his thinking and wit, with commentary amplifying his insightful observations.

President Reagan came into office during a very troubling time: 1981. The economy was suffering from "stagflation" (high unemployment accompanied by high inflation). Worldwide we were in the grips of the Cold War with the Soviet Union and other communist countries. Iran was holding our embassy staff hostage, yet our president was undaunted and led in a strong, optimistic, and effective manner. The hostages were quickly released, perhaps out of fear of the president's resolve.

Interestingly enough, the president's college major was economics, so when he applied "Reaganomics" (lower taxes and fewer regulations), the economy responded with solid growth, not just during his presidency, but for decades afterward.

In terms of the Cold War, President Reagan initiated "Star Wars" to create a nuclear warfare defense. The combination of superb leadership, fortitude, fruitful summit meetings, speeches ("Mr. Gorbachev, tear down this wall"), as well as the internal rot of communism, ended the Cold War without a shot being fired.

Vision for the Twenty-First Century

It is easy to say, "that was then and this is now." Yet we invite you to think about the similarities with the current situation. President Reagan had the vision to peer beyond the immediate disasters of the economy, the Cold War, and the

7

hostages in Iran. In the twenty-first century, we have similar challenges, including our troubled economy as well as wars in Iraq and Afghanistan and the War on Terror. Vision requires knowledge, imagination, and faith, all of which President Reagan had in abundance. We invite you to review some of this great president's quotations, along with our commentary. The commentary is meant to help amplify and assist in applying the president's wisdom to our times in simple, yet powerful ways. *Good Reading!*

John E. Wade II
Daniel P. Agatino

* * *

When John E. Wade II was searching for authors to contribute essays for inclusion in his book *How to Achieve a Heaven on Earth,* Pelican Publishing Company put him in touch with Daniel P. Agatino. Wade and Agatino's mutual interests and reciprocal respect led to friendship and now to this book.

Appointed to the Air Force Academy after high school, Wade received an honorable medical discharge and ultimately received his bachelor's and master's degrees in accounting from the University of Georgia. He was named the most outstanding senior accounting student and served as the president of Beta Alpha Psi, the accounting honor society. Wade worked in the private sector for nearly ten years and then for the federal government for twenty.

Wade's writing career picked up where his accounting career left off. The rights to his first book, *Focus Investing,* were purchased, though at the time the book was not published because of changing market conditions. Additionally, Wade has written many hundreds of essays on a wide range of topics, from love to politics, health, and happiness. In 2002 he published *Deep Within My Heart,* a collection of essays, several of which explored the 2000 presidential campaign. Wade was twice named Republican of the Year for the State of Louisiana, which he attributes, at least in part, to the essays he wrote during that time frame.

While traveling around the world, often on mission trips or spiritual journeys, Wade was inspired to collect essays that would address the question "what would it take to make a heaven on earth?" The resulting book was published in 2010, and some of these ideas inspired the television series *A World That Works*, which Wade is producing through his company, World10, Inc (www.World10.org).

Agatino's education and professional history is equally diverse. He received master's degrees in communication from William Paterson University and theology from the College of Saint Elizabeth, and both a *juris doctorate* and a PhD in communication from Rutgers University. He has taught courses in communication and law at numerous colleges and universities, including the College of Saint Elizabeth and Seton Hall University, School of Law. Currently Agatino practices criminal defense and entertainment law.

In addition to his academic and professional publications, Agatino compiled an assortment of quotations by President Reagan, which he shares in **The Tao of Reagan: Common Sense from an Uncommon Man,** published by Pelican. Not surprisingly, Agatino was happy to oblige Wade's request for an essay for inclusion in **How to Achieve a Heaven on Earth.** The various essays examine aspects of ten elements—peace, security, freedom, democracies, prosperity, spiritual harmony, racial harmony, ecological harmony, health, and moral purpose and meaning, as well as some individual paths to the goal— and Agatino's essay, "The Tao of Reagan," is included in the chapter on democracy.

Wade and Agatino eventually met in person when Agatino attended the **How to Achieve a Heaven on Earth** book launch event in New Orleans. A few months later, when Wade traveled to Boston, the two spent a day together discussing possible joint literary pursuits, including a revision of *Focus Investing* and Wade's memoirs. Their discussions continued in Costa Rica a few months after that, when Wade arranged for several essay authors to attend a motivational workshop.

Always contemplating new projects, in May 2011, Wade formed a creative brainstorming group, consisting of himself, Againto, and me. Almost immediately, Wade conceived the idea to pair the Reagan quotations contained in Agatino's book with commentary relating them to the twenty-first century and naturally Agatino was quite receptive. The wise words (and wisecracks) of President Reagan readily inspired Wade and Agatino. We now hope that this book will inspire you.

Charlotte Livingston
Editor

CHAPTER 1
America

Freedom Is the Right

"Freedom is the right to question and change the established way of doing things. It is the continuous revolution of the marketplace. It is the understanding that allows us to recognize shortcomings and seek solutions."
—Address at Moscow State University, May 31, 1988.

We have made great progress since President Reagan's comment, but I'm sure he would not have been satisfied until the whole world is free.   John E. Wade II (J. W.)

Here, the word "marketplace" can refer to commerce or the "marketplace of ideas" that fuels so much of our lives.
Daniel P. Agatino (D. A.)

You Don't Become President

"When people tell me I became president on January 20, 1981, I feel I have to correct them. You don't become president of the United States. You are given temporary custody of an institution called the presidency, which belongs to our people."
—Address to the Republican National Convention, August 15, 1988.

It is unfortunate when a great president leaves office, but it can be a worthwhile event when an inferior president leaves office.
J. W.

Reagan had such respect for the office of the presidency that he was never without a jacket and tie when in the Oval Office.
D. A.

Government Has No Power

"We are a nation that has a government—not the other way around. And this makes us special among the nations of the Earth. Our government has no power except that granted it by the people. It is time to check and reverse the growth of government which shows signs of having grown beyond the consent of the governed."

—Inaugural Address, January 20, 1981.

These words are especially appropriate for the twenty-first century as we must shrink government and decrease debt.   J. W.

In the old days it was believed God gave his power to a monarch who then shared it, sparingly, with princes, who shared a bit with dukes, who passed a bit on to knights. Eventually, some small agency passed it to the common people. Reagan believed the success of the USA is grounded in the inversion of this formula. He believed we all have the same God-given rights and the leaders serve at the pleasure of the people.   D. A.

Springtime of Hope

"In this springtime of hope, some lights seem eternal;
America's is."
> —Republican National Committee speech,
> August 23, 1984.

Optimism must be the eternal flame of America.   J. W.

We would do well to have a renewed "springtime of hope."
> D. A.

A Special Interest Group

"We hear much of special interest groups. Our concern must be for a special interest group that has been too long neglected. It knows no sectional boundaries or ethnic and racial divisions, and it crosses political party lines. It is made up of men and women who raise our food, patrol our streets, man our mines and our factories, teach our children, keep our homes, and heal us when we are sick—professionals, industrialists, shop keepers, clerks, cabbies, and truck drivers. They are, in short, 'We the people,' this breed called Americans."

—Inaugural address, January 20, 1981.

The American people must always be first and foremost on the minds of all public officials.   J. W.

Again we see Reagan's recognition that America's greatness is inextricably tied to the people.   D. A.

Our Capacity for Self-government

"This is the issue of this election: whether we believe in our capacity for self-government or whether we abandon the American Revolution and confess that a little intellectual elite in a far-distant capital can plan our lives for us better than we can plan for ourselves."
—Nationally televised speech for presidential candidate Barry Goldwater, Los Angeles, California, October 27, 1964.

Our capacity for self-government is just as essential in the twenty-first century as when President Reagan uttered these words decades ago. J. W.

Reagan was not being anti-intellectual, for he was himself a very smart man. Instead, he was critical of those who sought to impose their grand visions on a people perfectly capable of taking care of themselves. D. A.

The States Created the Federal Government

"All of us need to be reminded that the federal government did not create the states, the states created the federal government. . . . Steps will be taken aimed at restoring the balance between the various levels of government."

—Inaugural address, January 20, 1981.

The Tenth Amendment to the Constitution of the United States limits the power of the federal government. Its application was hotly debated in Reagan's time and continues, perhaps even more so, into our present day.   D. A.

Strong American Influence

"It was leadership here at home that gave us strong American influence abroad, and the collapse of imperial Communism. Great nations have responsibilities to lead, and we should always be cautious of those who would lower our profile, because they might just wind up lowering our flag."
—Republican National Committee Annual Gala, February 3, 1994.

We must lead with the realization that a global reality is here for good. J. W.

Reagan wanted America to be a world leader and his policies showed he envisioned us more as the world's firefighters than the world's police; we don't keep the peace, but we do put out the fires. D. A.

The Cause of Freedom

"The years ahead will be great ones for our country, for the cause of freedom and the spread of civilization. The West will not contain Communism; it will transcend Communism. We will not bother to denounce it; we'll dismiss it as a sad, bizarre chapter in human history whose last pages are even now being written."
—Speech at University of Notre Dame, May 17, 1981.

President Reagan's wise words reflected a reality that few saw at that time.   J. W.

How prophetic were the words, "We will not bother to denounce it; we'll dismiss it as a sad, bizarre chapter in human history." One wonders what bizarre experiments Reagan would dismiss in our own age.   D. A.

This Blessed Land Was Set Apart

"I've always believed that this blessed land was set apart in a special way, that some divine plan placed this great continent here between the two oceans to be found by people from every corner of the Earth—people who had a special love for freedom and the courage to uproot themselves, leave their homeland and friends to come to a strange land. And, when coming here, they created something new in all the history of mankind—a country where man is not beholden to government; government is beholden to man."
—Address given at the National Religious Broadcasters convention, January 31, 1983.

Our nation is special and our government should always express the will of the people rather than the other way around. J. W.

Although these words echo sentiments of Manifest Destiny, Reagan did realize that history, including American history, has both a good and bad story to tell. We are not all glory and honor, but an element of our greatness is to repent and restore. D. A.

Our Best Effort

"The crisis we are facing today . . . does require, however, our best effort, and our willingness to believe in ourselves, and to believe in our capacity to perform great deeds; to believe that together, with God's help, we can and will resolve the problems which now confront us. And after all, why shouldn't we believe that? We are Americans. God bless you, and thank you."
　　　　　—First Inaugural Address, January 20, 1981.

We are American citizens, but we are also world citizens. J. W.

Studies show that we Americans like our presidents to be religious, but not too religious. Reagan was unashamed of his faith but recognized a distinction between personal faith and official duty.　　　　　D. A.

Faith of Our People

"Throughout our history, Americans have put their faith in God, and no one can doubt that we have been blessed for it. The earliest settlers of this land came in search of religious freedom. Landing on a desolate shoreline, they established a spiritual foundation that has served us ever since. It was the hard work of our people, the freedom they enjoyed and their faith in God that built this country and made it the envy of the world. In all of our great cities and towns evidence of the faith of our people is found: Houses of worship of every denomination are among the oldest structures."
—Proclamation issued on National Day of Prayer, March 19, 1981.

I believe God is leading all of humanity to a heaven on earth with His enduring, steadfast love. J. W.

The history of old Europe is fraught with religiously inspired wars and aggression. The United States has managed to avoid this type of sectarian violence, in part, because, as Reagan mentioned, we are free to follow any faith or none at all. D. A.

America, the Last Best Hope

"The explicit promise in the Declaration that we're endowed by our Creator with certain inalienable rights was meant for all of us. It wasn't meant to be limited or perverted by special privilege or by double standards. . . . Trusting in God and helping one another, we can and will preserve the dream of America, the last best hope of man on earth."
—Speech given at the annual meeting of the American Bar Association, Atlanta, Georgia, August 1, 1983.

Trusting in God can help us preserve the dream of America and spread the goal of a heaven on earth throughout the world, which shall include: peace, security, freedom, democracies, prosperity, spiritual harmony, racial harmony, ecological harmony, and health as well as moral purpose and meaning. J. W.

Reagan's line about "helping one another" can be understood as a recognition that God gave us certain rights, but they come with certain responsibilities. D. A.

Purpose to Our National Existence

"So, you can see why, to me, the story of these last eight years and this presidency goes far beyond any personal concerns. It is a continuation, really, of a far larger story, a story of a people and a cause: a cause that, from our earliest beginnings, has defined us as a nation and given purpose to our national existence. The hope of human freedom, the quest for it, the achievement of it, is the American saga."
—Final radio address as president, January 14, 1989.

Freedom is alive in the twenty-first century. We must seek a world full of robust, stable, prosperous democracies. Then we will have worldwide peace and freedom. J. W.

This final radio address echoes a theme consistent in Reagan's life from his earliest days in politics. Freedom is the defining characteristic of America and when we give it up, or exchange it for some other perceived good, we are gambling away our very way of life. D. A.

Freedom Is Fragile

"Freedom is a fragile thing and is never more than one generation away from extinction. It is not ours by inheritance; it must be fought for and defended constantly by each generation, for it comes only once to a people. Those who have known freedom and then lost it have never known it again."
—Inaugural Address as Governor of California, January 5, 1967.

Historically, many have secured and maintained freedom through force. But it doesn't have to be that way. Gandhi and his fellow countrymen established their freedom through nonviolence, and there are other examples of such means. However, the United States plays a special role in helping to guide our globe peacefully through strength. The end result will be freedom, not just in our times, but permanently for our entire world. J. W.

It is very easy to fall prey to the false notion that the freedoms guaranteed to us by the United States Constitution are unassailable. Freedom is not earned once and for all but must be claimed and sometimes even won in a fight. In a democracy, happily, that fight is usually played out in the courts and the marketplace of ideas and not on a battlefield. D. A.

CHAPTER 2
The Economy

If Not Us, Who?

"An almost unbroken fifty years of deficit spending has finally brought us to a time of reckoning. We have come to a turning point, a moment for hard decisions. I have asked the Cabinet and my staff a question, and now I put the same question to all of you: If not us, who? And if not now, when? It must be done by all of us going forward with a program aimed at reaching a balanced budget. We can then begin reducing the national debt."
—Second Inaugural Address, January 21, 1985.

This is the same question we must ask ourselves. Only now, we have our backs to the wall as the present and the future depend on actions beyond anything ever done concerning fiscal responsibility.   J. W.

"If not us, who? And if not now, when?" No better words can guide us through our current challenges.   D. A.

Still Get Rich

"We're the party that wants to see an America in which people can still get rich."
—Said at the Republican Congressional Dinner, Washington, D.C., May 4, 1982.

Republicans believe in opportunity for all.   J. W.

In an era during which talk of the redistribution of wealth is more acceptable than in days past we would do well to remember that while freedom and wealth are not synonymous, they are symbiotic.   D. A.

Deficit Upon Deficit

"For decades, we have piled deficit upon deficit, mortgaging our future and our children's future for the temporary convenience of the present. To continue this long trend is to guarantee tremendous social, cultural, political, and economic upheavals. You and I, as individuals, can, by borrowing, live beyond our means, but for only a limited period of time. Why, then, should we think that collectively, as a nation, we are not bound by that same limitation?"
—First Inaugural Address, January 20, 1981.

In the twenty-first century, we must take responsibility fiscally; or else we could experience a decade or two of no growth, like Japan, or hyperinflation, like Germany, after World War I.

J. W.

Here is yet another example of how Reagan applied common sense to perplexing problems. He cut through the rhetoric to explain that the country, like individuals, must spend within limits.

D. A.

We Spend Too Much

"We don't have a trillion-dollar debt because we haven't taxed enough; we have a trillion-dollar debt because we spend too much."

—Address to National Association of Realtors,
March 28, 1982.

In the twenty-first century, President Reagan's words are still true—we spend too much. J. W.

These words were spoken when the term "trillion-dollar" was shocking. Now it seems commonplace to discuss multi-trillion dollar debts without raising an eyebrow. D. A.

The Founding Fathers Knew

"The Founding Fathers knew a government can't control the economy without controlling people. And they knew when a government sets out to do that, it must use force and coercion to achieve its purpose."
—Nationally televised speech for presidential candidate Barry Goldwater, Los Angeles, California, October 27, 1964.

This may seem naive to us today, because we live in a global economy that demands some regulation to ensure equity and safety. But Reagan was not a libertarian who wanted to do away with any and all government oversight; he did, however, wish to limit the power that the government has over commerce. D. A.

Our Birthright as Citizens

"We believed then and now: There are no limits to growth and human progress, when men and women are free to follow their dreams. And we were right to believe that. Tax rates have been reduced, inflation cut dramatically and more people are employed than ever before in our history. We are creating a nation once again vibrant, robust, and alive. There are many mountains yet to climb. We will not rest until every American enjoys the fullness of freedom, dignity, and opportunity as our birthright. It is our birthright as citizens of this great republic."
—Second Inaugural Address, January 21, 1985.

The type of leadership that President Reagan provided is needed now in this critical time. We must hope and pray that a Republican presidential candidate will step forward, win, and bring our nation through these treacherous waters. J. W.

Reagan knew that for freedom to be really meaningful, it cannot be possessed by only a select few, or even a mere majority, but is the "birthright" of each and every one of us. D. A.

The Size of the Federal Budget

"The size of the federal budget is not an appropriate barometer of social conscience or charitable concern."
—Address to the National Alliance of Business, October 5, 1981.

Enormous federal expenditures must be drastically scaled back in a kind way where federal employees who have been laid off will be assisted in pursuing fruitful careers in the private sector.

J. W.

Throwing money at a problem, no matter how noble the intent, did not work then and will not work now.

D. A.

Administration's Objective

"This Administration's objective will be a healthy, vigorous, growing economy."
—First Inaugural Address, January 20, 1981.

President Reagan did what he set out to do. Now we need to make drastic changes to reach fiscal viability. Our first goal should be to establish a sound economy in the United States, and then we should work throughout the world for peace, security, freedom, democracies, prosperity, spiritual harmony, racial harmony, ecological harmony, and health as well as moral purpose and meaning. J. W.

Begin to tie the threads of Reagan's words together and we find that a strong and robust nation is tied to a free people encouraged to engage in creative and entrepreneurial endeavors to the benefit of themselves, their neighbors, and the world.
D. A.

Welfare's Purpose

"Welfare's purpose should be to eliminate, as far as possible, the need for its own existence."
—*Los Angeles Times,* January 7, 1970.

I agree that providing the incentives and means for persons to get off welfare and earn a living is a worthy purpose.   J. W.

Reagan saw welfare as a safety net and not a permanent way of life.   D. A.

The People's Business

"Government is the people's business and every man, woman and child becomes a shareholder with the first penny of tax paid."
—Address to the New York City Partnership Association, January 14, 1982.

This should not persuade us that the more shares we hold (i.e. the more taxes we pay) the more American we are, but instead, the mere fact that we participate in a government of the people entitles us to a voice in its creation and function. D. A.

No Limits on Human Capacity

"There are no such things as limits to growth,
because there are no limits on the human capacity for
intelligence, imagination and wonder."
—Speech given to the University of South Carolina,
Columbia, September 20, 1983.

*Reagan believed in the limitless potential of the human mind,
especially when fostered in the land of freedom. Those who
argue that we will run out of new ideas and new inventions are
unimaginative.*   D. A.

The Problem

"Government is not the solution, it's the problem."
—Inaugural address, January 20, 1981.

This is especially true now as our government faces a crisis unknown in its history, or for that matter, the history of the world. Never before has the world's largest economy also had the largest debt. J. W.

This is reminiscent of Winston Churchill's quip about democracy being the worst form of government, except for all those other forms. D. A.

Daily Mugging

"The current tax code is a daily mugging."
—Labor Day Address, Independence, Missouri,
September 2, 1985.

*I certainly agree with President Reagan. We now need a simple,
prudent, low tax—properly defined so that it is understandable
to ordinary citizens.*   J. W.

*Reagan often discussed problems with our system of taxing, but
it is not within the power of the president to unilaterally amend
the tax code.*   D. A.

Government Is Like a Baby

"Government is like a baby—an alimentary canal with a big appetite at one end and no sense of responsibility at the other."
—Campaign for governor of California, as quoted in the *New York Times Magazine*, November 14, 1965.

As President Reagan was aware of the irresponsibility of the federal government in the 1960s, he would cringe at the budget deficits exceeding a trillion dollars a year and a debt in excess of $50,000 per person. This is not sustainable for long. J. W.

President Reagan was a master at discussing serious issues in a humorous manner. Here we see his concern over big government. These comments date back to the mid-sixties, so imagine what he would have to say about the size of our current federal government. D. A.

A Time for Choosing

"The Founding Fathers knew a government can't control the economy without controlling people. And they knew when a government sets out to do that, it must use force and coercion to achieve its purpose. So we have come to a time for choosing."

—October 27, 1964.

President Reagan believed deeply in freedom for the American people and, for that matter, for people around the world. When freedom rings globally, peace will reign. A world full of robust, stable, prosperous democracies will be one that enjoys lasting peace. I believe such a world will come about in the twenty-first century, sooner rather than later.   J. W.

President Reagan spoke these words when the United States was less reliant on the global economy. However, the internationalization of business and commerce is not an excuse for overly-burdensome government regulations. While some oversight is necessary, the most fertile ground for financial success is the free market.   D. A.

CHAPTER 3
God

Divine Guidance

"May all of you as Americans never forget your heroic origins, never fail to seek divine guidance and never lose your natural, God-given optimism."
—Speech to Republican National Convention, August 17, 1992.

We need divine guidance and God-given optimism now more than ever.   J. W.

Optimism is a theme that resonates throughout much of Reagan's speeches and even more of his actions!   D. A.

Shining City on a Hill

"Let us resolve tonight that young Americans will always
. . . find there a city of hope in a country that is free.
. . . And let us resolve they will say of our day and our
generation, we did keep the faith with our God, that we
did act worthy of ourselves, that we did protect and pass
on lovingly that shining city on a hill."
—Election-eve speech, November 3, 1980.

*These words need to echo now in the twenty-first century.
Freedom and faith are needed now on "that shining city on a
hill."*   J. W.

Under God

"Government growing beyond our consent had become a lumbering giant, slamming shut the gates of opportunity, threatening to crush the very roots of our freedom. What brought America back? The American people brought us back—with quiet courage and common sense; with undying faith that in this nation under God the future will be ours, for the future belongs to the free."

—State of the Union Address, February 4, 1986.

President Reagan was modest. His leadership brought the nation back. Now we need to lower corporate taxes and other taxes to be competitive worldwide. This would jump-start the economy, especially if tax codes are greatly simplified.   J. W.

Profound Moral Difference

"The men of Normandy had faith that what they were doing was right, faith that they fought for all humanity, faith that a just God would grant them mercy on this beachhead or the next. It was the deep knowledge—and pray God we have not lost it—that there is a profound moral difference between the use of force for liberation and the use of force for conquest."
—Speech commemorating D-Day Invasion given in Normandy, France, June 6, 1984.

President Reagan worked wonders in the Cold War without firing a shot. Mahatma Gandhi's peaceful methods and better use of United Nations diplomacy, as opposed to combat, should be utilized when at all possible. When combat is needed, the United States might handle the initial assault, but other nations should handle the occupation until a democracy is established. J. W.

Touch the Face of God

"We will never forget them, nor the last time we saw them—this morning, as they prepared for their journey, and waved good-bye, and 'slipped the surly bonds of earth' to 'touch the face of God.'"
—Speech on the *Challenger* disaster, given from the Oval Office of the White House, January 28, 1986.

These astronauts willingly risked their lives to explore space. Let us not give up that quest.   J. W.

The Will of God

"At every crucial turning point in our history Americans have faced and overcome great odds, strengthened by spiritual faith. The Plymouth settlers triumphed over hunger, disease, and a cruel Northern wilderness because, in the words of William Bradford, 'They knew they were Pilgrims, so they committed themselves to the will of God and resolved to proceed.' George Washington knelt in prayer at Valley Forge and in the darkest days of our struggle for independence said that 'the fate of unborn millions will now depend, under God, on the courage and conduct of this army.' Thomas Jefferson, perhaps the wisest of our founding fathers, had no doubt about the source from which our cause was derived. 'The God who gave us life,' he declared, 'gave us liberty.' And nearly a century later, in the midst of a tragic and at times seemingly hopeless Civil War, Abraham Lincoln vowed that 'this nation, under God, shall have a new birth of freedom.'"

—Delivered during a radio broadcast to the nation,
September 18, 1982.

A great leader, President Reagan explains in eloquent words the presence of God throughout our history. God remains with us and I believe will see us through, somehow, some day, to a heaven on earth. **J. W.**

That Single Book

"We're blessed to have its words of strength, comfort, and truth. I'm accused of being simplistic at times with some of the problems that confront us. But I've often wondered: Within the covers of that single Book are all the answers to all the problems that face us today, if we'd only look there. 'The grass withereth, the flower fadeth, but the word of our God shall stand forever.' I hope Americans will read and study the Bible in 1983. It's my firm belief that the enduring values, as I say, presented in its pages have a great meaning for each of us and for our nation. The Bible can touch our hearts, order our minds, refresh our souls."

—Address given at the National Religious Broadcasters convention, January 31, 1983.

I believe God is present moment by moment within what I refer to as a "little piece of God" in each of us and all of us, since the dawn of humankind.   J. W.

God Back In

"If we get the federal government out of the classroom, maybe we'll get God back in."
—*Washingtonian Magazine,* July 1976.

Wisdom is made up of comprehensive knowledge and the positive values of honesty, compassion, and justice. These values should not be left out of our twenty-first century classrooms. J. W.

Lord Calls Me Home

"In closing let me thank you, the American people, for giving me the great honor of allowing me to serve as your president. When the Lord calls me home, whenever that may be, I will leave with the greatest love for this country of ours and eternal optimism for its future. I now begin the journey that will lead me into the sunset of my life. I know that for America there will always be a bright dawn ahead."

—Speech announcing he had Alzheimer's disease,
November 5, 1994.

President Reagan was a great human being. He was genuine and a natural, hard-thinking leader who had a wonderful understanding of our nation and the world.   J. W.

Most Heartening Signs

"As far as I'm concerned, the growth of religious broadcasting is one of the most heartening signs in America today."
—Address given at the National Religious Broadcasters convention, January 31, 1983.

President Reagan believed that a strong faith helped to ensure a robust respect for freedom. He subscribed to the idea set forth in the Declaration of Independence that all humans "are endowed by their Creator with certain unalienable rights." D.A.

Jesus Can Lift Our Hearts

"Think of it: the most awesome military machine in history, but it is no match for that one, single man, hero, strong yet tender, Prince of Peace. His name alone, Jesus, can lift our hearts, soothe our sorrows, heal our wounds, and drive away our fears. He gave us love and forgiveness. He taught us truth and left us hope. In the Book of John is the promise that we all go by—'For God so loved the world that He gave His only begotten Son, that whosoever believeth in Him should not perish, but have everlasting life.'"

—Address given at the National Religious Broadcasters convention, January 31, 1983.

Again we see that Reagan was not shy about his faith. But notice his point about the futility of the Imperial Roman war machine.

D. A.

In God We Trust

"Our Nation's motto—'In God We Trust'—was not chosen lightly. It reflects a basic recognition that there is a divine authority in the universe to which this nation owes homage."
—National Day of Prayer Proclamation, March 19, 1981.

I agree that our nation is pledged to Almighty God. As such, each of us and all of us must listen for Almighty God and that "little piece of God" within us and seek to do God's will in our lives.

J. W.

It is an interesting point. We do not proclaim in "luck," "fate," or "random chance," we trust.

D. A.

Protect Religious Values from Government

"To those who cite the First Amendment as reason for excluding God from more and more of our institutions and every-day life, may I just say: The First Amendment of the Constitution was not written to protect the people of this country from religious values; it was written to protect religious values from government tyranny."
—Speech given to the Alabama State Legislature, March 15, 1982.

President Reagan rightly explains that religious values ought to be protected. Prayer in schools seems like something that has wrongly been removed. Wisdom, comprised of comprehensive knowledge and positive values, should be the goal of what is taught in our schools. J. W.

Freedom of religion is not synonymous with freedom from religion. D. A.

The Nation Has Turned to God

"Through the storms of Revolution, Civil War, and the great World Wars, as well as during the times of disillusionment and disarray, the nation has turned to God in prayer for deliverance. We thank Him for answering our call, for, surely, He has. As a nation, we have been richly blessed with His love and generosity."
—Address given proclaiming a National Day of Prayer, February 12, 1982.

I agree with President Reagan, though I profoundly believe that God has, for each of us and all of us, an enduring and steadfast love. J. W.

It strikes me that a politically correct version of this and many other Reagan quotes would sound quite absurd. "We thank Him or Them or Her or possibly there is no one to thank." D. A.

CHAPTER 4
Pop Culture

More Fun Than Being President

"This is really more fun than being president. I really do love baseball and I wish we could do this on the lawn every day."

—Old-Timers' Game 1983.

President Reagan, I'm told, practically always had a smile on his face. He must have been smiling when he said the above words.

J. W.

Self-Delusion

"If history teaches anything, it teaches self-delusion in the face of unpleasant facts is folly."
—Speech to the House of Commons of the United Kingdom, June 8, 1982.

People are, in general, envious of others in better circumstances, whether or not those whom they envy have earned their position.

J. W.

Courage to Do What We Know Is Morally Right

"They say the world has become too complex for simple answers. They are wrong. There are no easy answers, but there are simple answers. We must have the courage to do what we know is morally right. Winston Churchill said that 'the destiny of man is not measured by material computation. When great forces are on the move in the world, we learn we are spirits—not animals.' And he said, 'There is something going on in time and space, and beyond time and space, which, whether we like it or not, spells duty.'"

—Nationally televised speech for presidential candidate
Barry Goldwater, Los Angeles, California,
October 27, 1964.

I like what President Reagan said—that there are no easy answers, but there are simple answers. Many will tell you that life is complex and thus life's problems require complex answers. I disagree. I believe a more intelligent person will come up with a simpler answer than a less astute person. J. W.

What I Take from the Past

"Now, as most of you know, I'm not one for looking back. I figure there will be plenty of time for that when I get old. But rather, what I take from the past is inspiration for the future, and what we accomplished during our years at the White House must never be lost amid the rhetoric of political revisionists."
—Republican National Committee Annual Gala,
February 3, 1994.

I consider President Regan to have been the greatest president to serve during my lifetime. It was my admiration for President Reagan that made me become a Republican. Although we will never have another quite like President Reagan, perhaps we will have the wisdom to elect an equally effective leader for our great country. J. W.

Paying for This

"I am paying for this microphone, Mr. Breen."
—New Hampshire Primary, 1980;
said after someone attempted to shut off
Reagan's microphone at a debate he funded.

President Reagan had a superb sense of humor along with his other wonderful qualities.   J. W.

Don't Inhale

"When you see all that rhetorical smoke billowing up
from the Democrats, well ladies and gentleman, I'd
follow the example of their nominee; don't inhale."
—Republican National Convention, 1992;
said in reference to Bill Clinton who admitted to
smoking marijuana but not inhaling.

*President Reagan, in my opinion, chose the right party for
himself, and largely because of him, I chose that same party.*

J. W.

*I, on the other hand, am a proud independent. Reagan attracted
many democrats ("Reagan Democrats") and independents.*

D. A.

The Reagan Revolution

"We've done our part. And as I walk off into the city streets, a final word to the men and women of the Reagan revolution, the men and women across America who for eight years did the work that brought America back. My friends: We did it. We weren't just marking time. We made a difference. We made the city stronger, we made the city freer, and we left her in good hands. All in all, not bad, not bad at all."
—Farewell Address to the Nation, January 20, 1989.

Thank you, President Reagan. You gave your best and you shined so brightly. May we hope for, and vote for, another bright spot in our country's leadership.   J. W.

History Teaches

"History teaches that wars begin when governments believe the price of aggression is cheap."
—Address to the nation, January 16, 1984.

President Reagan captured giant concepts in understandable ways. J. W.

Studying the Issues

"Are you willing to spend time studying the issues, making yourself aware, and then conveying that information to family and friends? Will you resist the temptation to get a government handout for your community? Realize that the doctor's fight against socialized medicine is your fight. We can't socialize the doctors without socializing the patients. Recognize that government invasion of public power is eventually an assault upon your own business. If some among you fear taking a stand because you are afraid of reprisals from customers, clients, or even government, recognize that you are just feeding the crocodile hoping he'll eat you last."

—Nationally televised speech for presidential candidate Barry Goldwater, Los Angeles, California, October 27, 1964.

In a democracy such as ours, voters have the privilege and duty to try to select wise, capable, and honest office holders.   J. W.

This is interesting advice, given our current healthcare debate.
D. A.

It's Hard to Dazzle Us

"We've grown used to wonders in this century. It's hard to dazzle us. But for twenty-five years the United States space program has been doing just that. We've grown used to the idea of space, and perhaps we forget that we've only just begun. We're still pioneers."
—Speech on the Challenger disaster, given from the Oval Office of the White House, January 28, 1986.

The space quest should continue and not be aborted, because through these missions we almost certainly will make awesome discoveries and technological advances.   J. W.

CHAPTER 5
Humor

Fourth of July

"Republicans believe every day is the Fourth of July, but Democrats believe every day is April 15."
                                    —*New York Times*, October 10, 1984.

Unfortunately, there's a lot of truth to President Reagan's statement.   J. W.

No doubt, Reagan's years in television and film helped him develop such wit.   D. A.

Make My Day

"I have only one thing to say to the tax increasers: Go ahead, make my day."
—Said in a speech promising to veto legislation proposing a tax hike, March 13, 1985.

One must admire President Reagan's resolve. If taxes could be lowered and simplified, our nation would be much more competitive in this twenty-first century global economy. J.W.

For readers unfamiliar with the quote, "Go ahead, make my day," it was uttered in a film around this time by Clint Eastwood's famous character Dirty Harry. D. A.

Recession Is

"Recession is when your neighbor loses his job.
Depression is when you lose yours. And recovery is when
Jimmy Carter loses his."
—Spoken sometime during the campaign against Jimmy
Carter, recalled at a dedication of Carter Presidential
Center in Atlanta, October 2, 1986.

*The above sounds like a joke and perhaps it was. But what
happened was true. A leader with vision is greatly needed right
now, in the twenty-first century, perhaps more so than during
President Reagan's era of great need.*   J. W.

*This is a pithy quote that can be reworked for any upcoming
election.*   D. A.

My Best Side

"Just remember my best side is my right side—my far right side."
—To White House News Photographers Association,
May 18, 1983.

On the political spectrum, conservatives lean right and liberals lean left. D. A.

Terrifying Words

"The nine most terrifying words in the English language
are, 'I'm from the government and I'm here to help.'"
—Discussing aid to farmers at a Chicago press
conference, August 12, 1986.

*Unfortunately, many governmental agencies are complex
and not fully understood by everyday citizens, including the
Internal Revenue Service. Simplifying these agencies and
systems (including the tax code) should be a top priority for our
government officials.*   J. W.

*Here is another humorous, but penetrating, revelation of
Reagan's distrust of the government's role of social engineer.*
D. A.

Anti-Communist

"How do you tell a Communist? Well, it's someone who reads Marx and Lenin. And how do you tell an anti-Communist? It's someone who understands Marx and Lenin."
—Remarks in Arlington, Virginia, September 25, 1987.

I truly thank God that the rot of Communism is almost gone, with only Cuba and North Korea still having centrally planned economies. J. W.

This is a great line and I'm surprised it was not reworked into a wisecrack about the difference between Democrats and Republicans. D. A.

Forgot

"Honey, I forgot to duck."
—Speaking to Nancy Reagan, his wife, while recovering
from a gunshot wound inflicted by John Hinckley on
March 30, 1981.

Because this occurred early in President Reagan's first term, had this attempt been successful, the country would not have benefitted from his many superb contributions. Such a loss would have been a true disaster and I thank God that we did not lose our president on that day. J. W.

The attempted assassination of the president and his subsequent reaction helped show the nation the depth of Reagan's character. D. A.

Hope

"I hope you're all Republicans."
—Speaking to surgeons before he was to undergo an
   operation for his gunshot wound, March 30, 1981.

*President Reagan was full of life even before a surgery that was
later determined to be critical to his survival.*   J. W.

*Even on the operating table, Reagan was the quintessential
showman.*   D. A.

Age an Issue

"I will not make age an issue in this campaign. I am not going to exploit for political purposes my opponent's youth and inexperience."
—Spoken by seventy-three-year-old Reagan to fifty-six-year-old Walter Mondale, October 21, 1984.

President Reagan was the consummate likeable politician. I remember when he made this statement in a presidential debate and even Walter Mondale couldn't help smiling about the remark.

J. W.

By offering this witty repartee Reagan inoculated his audience against anticipated criticisms of his old age. It was a clever move.

D. A.

Outlaw Russia

"My fellow Americans, I'm pleased to tell you today that I've signed legislation that will outlaw Russia forever. We begin bombing in five minutes."
—Joking while testing a microphone for Saturday broadcast, August 11, 1984.

It seems President Reagan's sense of humor knew no bounds.
J. W.

The aftermath of this gaffe was not a joking matter as some listeners took Reagan seriously. D. A.

That's Only Twenty-four

"I did turn seventy-five today—but remember, that's only 24 Celsius."
—Commenting on his birthday, February 6, 1986.

Wit does not always correspond with age, as there are many who never display a sense of humor. Such was not the case with President Reagan.   J. W.

This chapter on jokes could go on and on, because Reagan had a great sense of humor. Some criticized him for his mirth but those same dour commentators would have likely had the same reaction if he were stuffy and pompous.   D. A.

Why Take the Chance

"It's true hard work never killed anybody; but I figure, why take the chance?"
> —A favorite quip often used by the president.

The joke of course is that President Reagan's hard work led to many great accomplishments.   J. W.

In fact, Reagan was an incredibly industrious and hard-working president.   D. A.

I Was a Democrat

Reporter Sam Donaldson: "Mr. President, in talking about the continuing recession tonight, you have blamed the mistakes of the past and you've blamed Congress. Does any of the blame belong to you?" President Reagan: "Yes, because for many years I was a Democrat."

—Press Conference, 1982.

For those who suspect Reagan's humor is nothing more than good speech writing done by professionals, here is an off-the-cuff remark.   D. A.

If it Moves, Tax it

"Government's view of the economy could be summed up in a few short phrases: If it moves, tax it. If it keeps moving, regulate it. And if it stops moving, subsidize it."
                    —Remarks to the White House Conference on Small Business, August 15, 1986.

Unfortunately, that's the way a lot of Democrats think.   J. W.

Notice that Reagan was not placing blame solely on the opposition party, the Democrats, but on government in general.   D. A.

Like Show Business

"Politics is just like show business. You have a hell of an opening, you coast for a while, you have a hell of a closing."

—Attributed to President Reagan.

Actually, Reagan's terms in office allowed for very little coasting. A short outline of some of his greatest accomplishments can be found in the Introduction to this book.   D. A.

Write a Book

"Politics is not a bad profession. If you succeed there are many rewards; if you disgrace yourself you can always write a book."

—Attributed to President Reagan.

There are numerous books about Reagan and even some that record his own words.   D. A.

Middle-Aged Actor

"What makes him think a middle-aged actor, who's
played with a chimp, could have a future in politics?"
—Commenting on Clint Eastwood's candidacy to be
mayor of Carmel, California.

*For those who do not know, Reagan himself was an actor who
worked with a chimp in the film* Bedtime for Bonzo.   D. A.

Eternal Life

"I've always stated that the nearest thing to eternal life we'll ever see on this earth is a government program."
                                                —A remark made April 1986.

This is very true and especially disastrous when the federal debt, deficits, and future costs of Medicare, Medicaid, and Social Security are huge and onerous.   J. W.

It is not that government programs do not work; it is that they often become troublesome when they are created to last in perpetuity.   D. A.

Second Oldest Profession

"Politics is supposed to be the second oldest profession. I have come to realize that it bears a very close resemblance to the first."
—A remark made March 3, 1978.

He is of course referring to prostitution, which is often referred to as "the world's oldest profession."   D. A.

A Fella's Character

"You can tell a lot about a fella's character by whether he picks out all of one color or just grabs a handful."
—Telling why he often had a jar of jelly beans nearby during important meetings.

I'm not sure what is revealed by either choice, though I understand that Reagan's favorite flavor was licorice. D. A.

CHAPTER 6
Politics

Maximum of Individual Freedom

"You and I are told we must choose between a left or right, but I suggest there is no such thing as a left or right. There is only an up or down. Up to man's age-old dream—the maximum of individual freedom consistent with order—or down to the ant heap of totalitarianism. Regardless of their sincerity, their humanitarian motives, those who would sacrifice freedom for security have embarked on this downward path. Plutarch warned, 'The real destroyer of the liberties of the people is he who spreads among them bounties, donations and benefits.'"

—Nationally televised speech for presidential candidate
Barry Goldwater, Los Angeles, California,
October 27, 1964.

These sentiments held true in the days of antiquity with Plutarch, they were true when Reagan spoke them, and they will serve us well today.   D. A.

Political Landscape

"Although the political landscape has changed, the bold ideas of the 1980s are alive and well. . . . [A]nd as a result, it seems that our opponents have finally realized how unpopular liberalism really is. So now they're trying to dress their liberal agenda in a conservative overcoat."
—Republican Annual Gala, February 3, 1994.

President Clinton did try to use Republican ideas because they worked. We need to bring them forward in the twenty-first century.   J. W.

The debate between liberals and conservatives dates back to the origins of the United States. Alexander Hamilton held to certain liberal ideas compared to Thomas Jefferson, who believed in more conservative policies. Then, as now, citizens may prefer the goals of one party and the means of another. As a result, perhaps most citizens are actually "moderate."   D. A.

Do Away with Government

"It is not my intention to do away with government. It is rather to make it work—work with us, not over us; stand by our side, not ride on our back. Government can and must provide opportunity, not smother it; foster productivity, not stifle it."
—First Inaugural Address, January 20, 1981.

This is an extremely insightful statement: "Government can and must provide opportunity, not smother it; foster productivity, not stifle it." This certainly applies to the twenty-first century.

J. W.

This line is quintessential to Reagan's world view. It is also essential to our future. Government is necessary, but it is not sufficient.
D. A.

A Decade of Greed

"However, our task is far from over. Our friends in the other party will never forgive us for our success, and are doing everything in their power to rewrite history. Listening to the liberals, you'd think that the 1980s were the worst period since the Great Depression, filled with suffering and despair. I don't know about you, but I'm getting awfully tired of the whining voices from the White House these days. They're claiming there was a decade of greed and neglect, but you and I know better than that. We were there."
—Republican Annual Gala, February 3, 1994.

As with all eras, the 1980s had its share of good and bad news, but economically, Reagan's policy of lower taxes and limited government served to grow the economy. The same principles can serve us well now. D. A.

What Greater Service

"Public servants say, always with the best of intentions, 'What greater service we could render if only we had a little more money and a little more power.' But the truth is that outside of its legitimate function, government does nothing as well or as economically as the private sector."

—Nationally televised speech for presidential candidate Barry Goldwater, Los Angeles, California, October 27, 1964.

The reason our nation and government are in their current predicament is partially because of the government's creeping growth. The twenty-first century is in great need of an approach like President Reagan's, realizing that government is inefficient compared to the private sector. J. W.

Looking over the incredible advancements in science, technology, and culture in the past ten or twenty years, we find that the government, while not wholly absent from the process of innovation, was most helpful when taking on a limited role and letting private initiatives have the freedom to experiment, explore, and create. D. A.

Grand Larceny

"After watching the State of the Union address the other night, I'm reminded of the old adage that imitation is the sincerest form of flattery. Only in this case, it's not flattery, but grand larceny: the intellectual theft of ideas that you and I recognize as our own. Speech delivery counts for little on the world stage unless you have convictions, and, yes, the vision to see beyond the front row seats."
—Republican National Committee Annual Gala, February 3, 1994.

In reality, it does not matter if good ideas come from Republicans or Democrats. If they are good, and they work, let us put them into practice. The Jesuits have a saying about how a lot of good work can be done in this world if we are not too concerned about who gets the credit. **D. A.**

Humanitarian Goals

"Yet any time you and I question the schemes of the do-gooders, we're denounced as being opposed to their humanitarian goals. It seems impossible to legitimately debate their solutions with the assumption that all of us share the desire to help the less fortunate."
—Nationally televised speech for presidential candidate Barry Goldwater, Los Angeles, California, October 27, 1964.

In the twenty-first century, government solutions are being proposed in healthcare and to help big banks, which are in trouble because of their own mistakes.   J. W.

Reagan is arguing the classic "means" verse "ends" issue. Reagan took offense to the idea he was unconcerned with the plight of the poor and suffering simply because he realized government cannot solve all their problems.   D. A.

Arsenals of the World

"[N]o arsenal or no weapon in the arsenals of the world is so formidable as the will and moral courage of free men and women."
—First Inaugural Address, January 20, 1981.

Our country's people will always be its greatest strength. We must develop positive relationships with all of humanity. We must identify ourselves not only as Americans, but as world citizens. Our goal should be to have a world full of robust, stable, prosperous democracies—a world at peace.   J. W.

This proved true at the founding of our country; it was true at the fall of the Soviet Union; and the concept is essential for us in our current crisis.   D. A.

Ash Heap of History

"It is the Soviet Union that runs against the tide of history. . . . [It is] the march of freedom and democracy which will leave Marxism-Leninism on the ash heap of history as it has left other tyrannies which stifle the freedom and muzzle the self-expression of the people."
— Speech to Britain's Parliament, June 8, 1982.

President Reagan had great foresight. I believe that God intends for us to have peace, security, freedom, democracies, prosperity, spiritual harmony, racial harmony, ecological harmony, and health as well as moral purpose and meaning. J. W.

Some may read this and think, "not so fast, it looks like unfettered capitalism isn't so effective either." To them, Reagan would say, "Yes, that is correct." He never argued for a totally free society without law or regulation but instead fought for a freedom grounded in moral truth and an economy based on enlightened self-interest and even altruism but never selfishness.
D. A.

Delegate Authority

"Surround yourself with the best people you can find, delegate authority, and don't interfere."
—*Fortune Magazine*, September 15, 1986.

This is a quite simply put, yet very effective, way to lead. J. W.

Reagan was not afraid to surround himself with smart men and women. He also knew how to delegate without passing the buck, which is truly a difficult task. D. A.

Creating Bureaucracy

"We are for aiding our allies by sharing our material blessings with nations which share our fundamental beliefs, but we are against doling out money government to government, creating bureaucracy, if not socialism, all over the world."
—Nationally televised speech for presidential candidate Barry Goldwater, Los Angeles, California, October 27, 1964.

Reagan's words should make us rethink our role in international conflicts and nation-building.   D. A.

Socialized Medicine

"One of the traditional methods of imposing statism or socialism on a people has been by way of medicine. It's very easy to disguise a medical program as a humanitarian project; most people are a little reluctant to oppose anything that suggests medical care for people who possibly can't afford it."
—"Ronald Reagan Speaks Out Against Socialized Medicine" recording produced for the American Medical Association, 1961.

It is really amazing that the president's echo from the past is so appropriate to the legislation passed during Obama's presidency and a Congress controlled by Democrats. I believe that we should have universal health care; but, it is critical that it be structured in such a way that it makes economic sense. **J. W.**

Debates about the government's role in health care have raged for decades and show no sign of calming. Reagan was a humanitarian. However, he believed that a massive governmental oversight would inevitably bring about more harm than good.
D. A.

CHAPTER 7
Miscellaneous

Move Ahead

"We have to move ahead, but we are not going to leave anyone behind."
                    —Republican National Convention, July 1980.

We Republicans believe sincerely in opportunity for all.   J. W.

Both Democrats and Republicans claim to be the party of the people, and the challenge is to follow the above advice and move forward together and not at the exclusive expense of one group.
                                                    D. A.

Background Checks

"It's just plain common sense that there be a waiting period to allow local law enforcement officials to conduct background checks on those who wish to buy a handgun."
—Endorsing the Brady Handgun Violence Prevention Act, March 1991.

I agree with President Reagan that there should be a waiting period, especially for those wanting to purchase handguns and assault rifles or similar weapons. J. W.

This might be a surprising line coming from a conservative Republican, but Reagan was a pragmatist and not an ideologist.
D. A.

First Amendment

"Well, it might interest those critics to know that none other than the Father of our Country, George Washington, kissed the Bible at his inauguration. And he also said words to the effect that there could be no real morality in a society without religion. . . . So, when I hear the first amendment used as a reason to keep the traditional moral values away from policymaking, I'm shocked. The first amendment was not written to protect people and their laws from religious values; it was written to protect those values from government tyranny."

—Address given at the National Religious Broadcasters convention, January 31, 1983.

Religious values are the cornerstone of character, essential for our country to function properly. We have just experienced a financial meltdown because of all the missteps and greed in the mortgage industry. People of good character would not have allowed that debacle.   J. W.

Arms Race

"A (nuclear weapons) freeze now would be a very dangerous fraud, for that is merely the illusion of peace. The reality is that we must find peace through strength. . . . I urge you to beware the temptation of pride, the temptation of blithely declaring yourselves above it all and label both sides equally at fault, to ignore the facts of history and the aggressive impulses of an evil empire, to simply call the arms race a giant misunderstanding and thereby remove yourself from the struggle between right and wrong and good and evil."
—Speech to the National Association of Evangelicals, March 1983.

Even now we must sometimes apply "strength" in order to find peace; though, world peace will be achieved when our planet consists of robust, stable, prosperous democracies. J. W.

It was controversial for Reagan to label the Soviet Union as an "Evil Empire" but he truly believed that it was evil for a government to deny its people basic freedoms. Although such a label may have lacked diplomatic sensitivity, it was certainly unambiguous. D. A.

Tear Down this Wall

"If you seek peace, if you seek prosperity for the Soviet Union and Eastern Europe, if you seek liberalization: Come here, to this gate. Mr. Gorbachev, open this gate. Mr. Gorbachev, tear down this wall."
                    —Speech at the Berlin Wall, June 12, 1987.

President Reagan had great insight. In the twenty-first century we must strive for a heaven on earth with God's enduring, steadfast love.   J. W.

This last clause, "Mr. Gorbachev, tear down this wall," is among Reagan's most famous lines. I cannot help but wonder whether, if Reagan were still alive, he would make a similar challenge for us to tear down walls, metaphorically, that close us in and limit our freedoms.   D. A.

Your Dreams

"Your dreams, your hopes, your goals are going to be the dreams, the hopes, and the goals of this administration, so help me God."
—First Inaugural Address, January 20, 1981.

My hopes, dreams, goals, and fervent prayers are for a heaven on earth.   **J. W.**

Always a man of the people, Reagan had his own agenda to promote, but he sought to do so in conjunction with the dreams and goals of the American people. Too often, we see modern politicians pick and choose which groups they want to promote and which dreams and goals they will ignore.   **D. A.**

I Love You

"If I ache, it's because we are apart and yet that can't be, because you are inside and a part of me, so we really aren't apart at all. Yet I ache but wouldn't be without the ache, because that would mean being without you and that I can't be because I love you."

—1963 love letter written to his wife, Nancy Reagan, quoted in her book, *I Love You, Ronnie*, 2000.

President Reagan had a wonderful marriage and I believe that helped him become a great president. Such a match might be something to look for in our leaders of the twenty-first century. Politicians are still people and having a healthy marriage could help to ensure their outstanding performance.   J. W.

This is a rare look into the intimacy of the man we knew as the president and whom Nancy knew as a husband and best friend.
D. A.

Choose the Laws

"We cannot, as citizens, pick and choose the laws we will or will not obey."
    —Remarks made after Reagan ordered the firing of striking air-traffic controllers, September 3, 1981.

President Reagan made his mark early as a strong president, and it served him well in dealing with the Soviet Union, Congress, and others. Strength of character is an essential quality for an outstanding president to possess, now in the twenty-first century, as it always has been.   J. W.

Despite his disagreement with certain government laws and policies, Reagan did not counsel anarchy. Until and unless a law is changed, it must be obeyed; unless, as Dr. Martin Luther King pointed out, some higher law requires us to peacefully protest.

D. A.

The Party of Lincoln

"And let me add, in the party of Lincoln, there is no
room for intolerance and not even a small corner for
anti-Semitism or bigotry of any kind. Many people are
welcome in our house, but not the bigots."
—Acceptance speech given at the Republican National
Convention, August 23, 1984.

*The Republican Party continues in the twenty-first century to
welcome all citizens except bigots.*   J. W.

*America is a diverse nation and though in Reagan's time we
may have strived to be a giant melting pot with various cultures
merging together, today we are more of a salad. A salad can
have many different ingredients and still maintain itself as a
unified dish.*   D. A.

We Condemn It

"America's view of apartheid is simple and straightforward: We believe it is wrong. We condemn it. And we are united in hoping for the day when apartheid will be no more."
—Remarks made September 9, 1985.

Racial harmony is one of the ten elements that I have identified as essential to a heaven on earth. Much progress has been made, yet there is still work ahead. J. W.

Although his straightforward talk sometimes got him in hot water, Reagan was unapologetic in expressing his views on important issues such as apartheid. D. A.

Guns

"As long as there are guns, the individual that wants a gun for a crime is going to have one and going to get it. The only person who's going to be penalized and have difficulty is the law-abiding citizen, who then cannot have [it] if he wants protection."
—White House interview, March 22 1986.

Guns, religious expression, free speech; all these rights have been hotly debated since the country's inception. They will continue to be a source of controversy in the future. What Reagan reminds us is that we do not live in a perfect society; therefore, in order to make sensible laws, both the noblest and worst in our society need to be factored into the equation.   D. A.

Win One for the Gipper

"Someday when things are tough, maybe you can ask
the boys to go in there and win just one for the Gipper."
—Perhaps Reagan's most famous movie lines
spoken while playing George Gipp in the film
Knute Rockne, All American, 1940.

President Reagan won a host of victories for the Gipper! J. W.

*It would be difficult to find a future president who could capture
Reagan's mannerisms and charisma coupled with his political
savvy.* D. A.

Render Nuclear Weapons Obsolete

"For decades, we and the Soviets have lived under the threat of mutual assured destruction; if either resorted to the use of nuclear weapons, the other could retaliate and destroy the one who had started it. Is there either logic or morality in believing that if one side threatens to kill tens of millions of our people, our only recourse is to threaten killing tens of millions of theirs?
I have approved a research program to find, if we can, a security shield that would destroy nuclear missiles before they reach their target. It wouldn't kill people, it would destroy weapons. It wouldn't militarize space, it would help demilitarize the arsenals of Earth. It would render nuclear weapons obsolete."
—Second Inaugural Address, January 21, 1985.

I believe that President Reagan's ultimate goal of abolishing nuclear weapons will come true because of God's enduring and steadfast love for each of us and all of us.   J. W.

Though Reagan was in favor of a smaller government, he knew the importance of a strong military. Given the recent turmoil around the globe, it appears that commitment must continue for both our benefit and for the good of the entire globe.   D. A.

No Known Diseases

"Cures were developed for which there were no known diseases."
—Remarks made about Congress and its budget, 1981.

This situation is more serious now than at any time in our nation's history. J. W.

In this analogy, diseases are comparable to the unwise use of the people's money. Now it seems Congress not only creates needless cures, but perhaps is, metaphorically, making new and worse diseases. D. A.

EPILOGUE

At this time, the United States and most of the developed world are severely challenged economically. I have read that in 1980, President Reagan also faced extreme economic difficulties—stagflation, which is high inflation (13.6 percent at that time) coupled with slow economic growth, and an unemployment rate of 7.2 percent. Through the 1981 Reagan tax cut, lowered government regulation, and astute cooperation with the Federal Reserve System, he tamed inflation and ignited a twenty-five-year boom (1982-2007).

We should seriously consider how Reagan created this economic boom and what can be done now to return to economic stability and growth. It is important to note that President Reagan's college major was economics. He also had a very admirable group of economic advisors—including Milton Friedman, a champion of free market solutions that won him the Nobel Prize and powered his ideas around the world; Alan Greenspan, who later guided pro-growth policies as chairman of the Federal Reserve Board; and Arthur Laffer, who conceived the Laffer Curve, which shows that increasing tax rates beyond a certain level will discourage economic growth and tend to result in decreased tax revenue.

In contrast, during his presidency, Barack Obama, who lacks a background in economics, relied upon economic advisors who felt that the federal government could spend its way out of debt, deficits, and unemployment. By the end of 2011, our country was saddled with enormous national debt (nearly $50,000 per person, according to various sources I have seen) and a federal budget deficit of more than one trillion dollars. Additionally, during this period of time, the U.S. faced high unemployment and escalating costs associated with entitlements such as Medicaid, Medicare, and Social Security. According to one report, the number of citizens depending on government assistance increased 23 percent during President Obama's term in office.

The Reagan-inspired solutions to our problems include the following:

- Reduce taxes by adopting a simple, low graduated-flat tax with income that is well defined and understandable. Basic personal deductions, such as charitable and mortgage interest, could be retained. This tax would replace the existing corporate and individual income taxes, Social Security payroll taxes, the estate and gift taxes, as well as a large number of other taxes. This form of taxation is now practiced in twenty-seven nations around the world, with more countries considering making this change.
- Restore the strong dollar by a long-term steady reduction of our federal debt. A major key to this urgent endeavor is to take fiscal control of entitlements. This could be done in a kind manner (providing sufficient advance notice and gradual reduction are two options); but, it must be done.
- Drastically streamline the federal government, not just to balance the budget, but to minimize unnecessary government activities. To reduce government debt a surplus is necessary—not just a balancing of the budget.
- Deregulate, especially in areas such as taxation, which can be controlled to a great degree by simplification. The new accounting-based regulations passed after the Enron scandal also ought to be repealed, because they are unnecessary and costly. These regulations inhibit businesses from locating in our country and even encourage corporations to list their stock outside our nation, hurting our stock exchange, employment, and related high-paying jobs. The banking legislation passed after the 2008 fiscal crisis should also be severely

simplified and largely repealed. Little positive impact on banks was derived and yet another huge mound of regulation was created.

President Reagan launched a boom with pro-growth policies that benefitted all citizens. It is incumbent upon each and every one of us to carefully consider any political candidate's ability and willingness to invoke the above solutions with vigor, fortitude, and determination.

John E. Wade II

June 9, 1982 *(Getty Images)*

FAREWELL NOTE

Ronald Wilson Reagan

February 6, 1911—June 5, 2004

I thank President Reagan for his enormous impact on our country, its people, and the world. His leadership restored our economy and helped bring freedom and democracy to many nations throughout the globe.

Personally, I feel a special bond to Reagan because he helped shape my thinking and he also taught me to be a Republican. I believe my vision of a heaven on earth is similar to the grand vision Reagan had for our country and the world.

With sincere appreciation, I bid farewell to President Ronald Reagan.

John E. Wade II

HOW TO ACHIEVE
A HEAVEN
ON EARTH

101 insightful essays from the world's greatest
thinkers, leaders, and writers

Barack Obama
David Brooks
Ted Turner
Nicholas D. Kristof
Leonard Pitts, Jr.
Marianne Williamson
Chris Rose
Al Gore

George Bush
Dale Brown
Tony Blair
Thomas L. Friedman
George Rodrigue
Paul Prudhomme
Poppy Tooker
and more

Edited by John E. Wade II

"A fascinating octopus of a book on global change, reaching in all directions at once." —*Library Journal*

How to Achieve a Heaven on Earth, a collection of essays written by various authors, promotes and instills ten key elements that will help our world reach a heaven on earth. Each essay reflects and elaborates upon one or more of the ten elements of a heaven on earth: peace, security, freedom, democracies, prosperity, spiritual harmony, racial harmony, ecological harmony, and health, as well as moral purpose and meaning. Conceived and edited by this book's commentator, John E. Wade II, *How to Achieve a Heaven on Earth* contains essays written by world leaders, a Nobel Prize winner, and other luminaries. It also contains essays by this book's other commentator, Daniel P. Agatino, on democracy, entitled "The Tao of Reagan," and by this book's editor, Charlotte Livingston, on racial harmony, entitled "Saints on the Playing Field."